A Day in the Life: Grass

Wildebeest

Louise Spilsbury

Heinemann
LIBRARY
Chicago, Illinois

www.heinemannraintree.com

Visit our website to find out more information about Heinemann-Raintree books.

To order:

☎ Phone 888-454-2279

🖥 Visit www.heinemannraintree.com to browse our catalog and order online.

©2011 Heinemann Library
an imprint of Capstone Global Library, LLC
Chicago, Illinois

Edited by Dan Nunn, Rebecca Rissman, Catherine Veitch, and Nancy Dickmann
Designed by Philippa Jenkins
Picture research by Mica Brancic
Originated by Capstone Global Library
Printed and bound in China by South China Printing Company Ltd

14 13 12 11 10
10 9 8 7 6 5 4 3 2 1

Library of Congress Cataloging-in-Publication Data
Spilsbury, Louise.
  Wildebeest / Louise Spilsbury.
    p. cm. — (A day in the life. Grassland animals)
  Includes bibliographical references and index.
  ISBN 978-1-4329-4735-4 (hc) — ISBN 978-1-4329-4745-3 (pb) 1. Gnus—Juvenile literature. I. Title.
  QL737.U53S677 2011
  599.64'59—dc22   2010017851

Acknowledgments

We would like to thank the following for permission to reproduce photographs: FLPA pp. 5 (Minden Pictures/Richard Du Toit), 12, 13, 23 migrate (Minden Pictures/Suzi Eszterhas), 16 (© Winfried Wisniewski), 18 (Minden Pictures/Yva Momatiuk & John Eastcott); iStockphoto pp. 4 (© Norman Reid), 15 (© Robert Hardholt), 23 cheetah (© BostjanT); Nature Picture Library p. 21 (© Martin Dohrn); NHPA pp. 17, 23 female (© Woodfall/Joe McDonald); Photolibrary pp. 14, 23 male (Peter Arnold Images/Doug Cheeseman); Shutterstock pp. 6 (© Four Oaks), 7 (© Chris Fourie), 9, 23 herd (© Larsek), 10, 23 grassland (© wiw), 11, 23 watering hole (© Sebastien Burel), 19 (© Sergey Khachatryan), 20 (Johan Swanepoel), 22 (© Peter Betts), 23 hyena (© Antonio Jorge Nunes).

Cover photograph of a close-up portrait of a blue wildebeest, Etosha National Park, Namibia, reproduced with permission of Shutterstock (© Johan Swanepoel). Back cover photographs of (left) a wildesbeest's horns reproduced with permission of FLPA (Minden Pictures/Richard Du Toit) and (right) a wildesbeest calf reproduced with permission of FLPA (Winfried Wisniewski).

We would like to thank Michael Bright for his invaluable help in the preparation of this book.

The author would like to dedicate this book to her nephew and niece, Ben and Amelie: "I wrote these books for animal lovers like you. I hope you enjoy them". Aunty Louise.

Every effort has been made to contact copyright holders of material reproduced in this book. Any omissions will be rectified in subsequent printings if notice is given to the publisher.

Contents

Some words are in bold, **like this**. You can find out what they mean by looking in the glossary.

What Is a Wildebeest?

A wildebeest is a large animal that has a big head and long horns.

Wildebeests live together in groups called **herds**.

horns

Another name for a wildebeest is gnu.

This is because wildebeests sometimes make a loud "ga-nooo" sound!

What Do Wildebeests Look Like?

mane

A wildebeest has dark hair and a long, black mane.

It has a long tail and tough hooves on its feet.

male

female

An adult wildebeest is about as tall as a man's chest.

Males are bigger than **females**, and their horns are bigger.

Where Do Wildebeests Live?

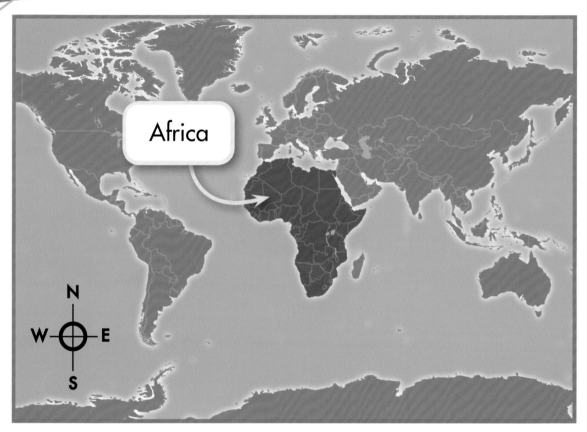

Africa

key: ■ = where wildebeests live

Wildebeests live in parts of eastern and southern Africa.

They live in places called **grasslands**.

In these grasslands, the land is covered in grasses and a few trees.

Most days it is hot and dry, but in some months it rains a lot.

What Do Wildebeests Do During the Day?

Most days, wildebeests wander around eating grass and other plants.

At midday when it gets very hot, they stand or lie down in a shady spot.

Wildebeests need to drink water once or twice a day.

That is why they never walk far away from a **watering hole**.

Why Do Wildebeests Migrate?

Wildebeests **migrate**, or move to another place, when it gets too hot.

They travel to places where there is water and green grass.

During the day, they walk a long way
and swim across rivers.

They return later, when it rains in the
grasslands again.

Why Do Wildebeests Fight?

Male wildebeests sometimes fight during the day to try to win a **female**.

They knock heads and horns until one of the animals gives up.

During the day males also guard an area of land.

They leave droppings, and the smell warns other males to keep off!

What Are Wildebeest Babies Like?

calf

Wildebeest calves have light-brown hair.

They can be born in the day or at night.

Calves drink milk from their mother, and soon eat grass too.

They can walk right away and follow the **herd**, day and night.

Which Animals Hunt Wildebeests?

crocodile

Lions, **cheetahs**, wild dogs, and **hyenas** hunt wildebeests on land.

Crocodiles may hide under water to catch wildebeests at rivers or **watering holes**.

When **herds** run from danger, calves stay safe in the middle of the group.

Females also attack or chase off animals that hunt their calves.

What Do Wildebeests Do at Night?

Wildebeests mostly rest and sleep at night.

Some wildebeests sleep while others look out for dangerous animals.

When wildebeests sleep they often lie on the ground in rows.

This gives them room to get up quickly if dangerous animals attack!

Wildebeest Body Map

horn

mane

tail

beard

hoof

Glossary

 **cheetah** large, spotted wild cat. A cheetah lives in Africa.

 **female** animal that can become a mother when it is grown up

 **grassland** land where mostly grasses grow

 **herd** large group of animals of one type, such as wildebeests

 **hyena** wild animal that mostly lives in grasslands in Africa. It looks like a dog.

 **male** animal that can become a father when it is grown up

 **migrate** move from one place to another

 **watering hole** pool of water that animals drink from

Find Out More

Books

Carney, Elizabeth. *Great Migrations: Whales, Wildebeests, Butterflies, Elephants, and Other Amazing Animals on the Move.* Des Moines, IA: National Geographic Children's Books, 2010.

Walden, Katherine. *Wildebeests (Safari Animals).* New York: PowerKids Press, 2009.

Websites

http://animals.nationalgeographic.com/animals/mammals/wildebeest.html

http://www.arkive.org/blue-wildebeest/connochaetes-taurinus/

Index